These Things Happen

Jennifer Harbertson

Presentation by *BookLeaf Publishing*

Web: www.bookleafpub.com

E-mail: info@bookleafpub.com

ISBN: 9789358738421

First edition 2023

To Dewan, Eben and Zander,

*May you rhyme on a whim in seriousness
and playfulness alike.*

ACKNOWLEDGEMENT

The lion's share of the credit for this should go to my mother for how she has made this happen through what can only be described as sheer will at some points along the timeline. She readied me for it by imparting knowledge, listening when it went wrong, always diligently reading, and providing encouragement. Sadly, her portion must now be split among the friends who keep me supplied with notebooks, such as Laura - my fellow Indigo veteran.

It should also go to the one who took up the mantle as a reader and opinion provider, even at a young age. Dewan, you were always raised to be her grandson; thank you for living up to the challenge.

Finally, to Steve, who has been my financial and moral support even though reading and writing are far beyond his comfort zone.

PREFACE

On a whim! That's how this book came into being. I recently told several children that I could rhyme on a whim and proceeded to prove that to them. Of course, poetry is not just about rhyme, although I often find the best rhymes in the last two lines of Shakespeare (making some daring claim) or Donaldson (where woodland creatures outwit dreamt-up villains). Poetry, I have known for years, is about the soul and I retreat with my books of poems when I feel particularly nostalgic or otherwise to entertain the children while they are eating their dinner. May this book inspire you to do both. Some poems are designed to speak to the hard stuff in life, others the whimsical. May the right kind find you in the right moment.

Penny For Your Thoughts

A penny for your thoughts or a pretty bow to tie
Around a wondering or pondering, you've
plucked out from the sky.

Tuppence for your opinion or comment on the
theme
Of whatever topic fashionable, or political or
dream.

Sixpence for your wisdom, sixpence for your
word
It won't matter in the least if it turns out to be
absurd.

Half crown for your answer, sober and sincere
We would not be the same without your mind,
my dear.

A pound for your advice, but only as an expert
But hold back if they would or can cause any
kind of hurt.

A penny for your thoughts, a penny for your
mind
But no one wants to hear it if you are not going
to be kind.

Dread nothing

Dread nothing in the ever-dark corners of the
world
Fear nothing in the caverns, cracks and crevices
laying curled
Beyond your eyes, but to your ears, their subtle
sounds are heard
Like the feelings of their scratching claws that in
your heart are stirred
The steady, deepened sound of every raspy
breath
The ungainly, grim and grizzly growl that
threatens certain death.

Put away all thoughts that monsters linger just
beyond your grasp

That if you were to move too loudly or even
were to gasp
They suddenly would leap from the thinness of
the air
And attack you so ferociously that you never
more would dare
To venture out of the safety, silence, and
simpleness of home
And in the wide world wander, finding new
places to roam.
Dread nothing in the ever-dark corners of the
world
For if you dread the things that might appear
within a swirl
Of sudden sights and booming blasts or rib-cage
ripping roars
For if you do not dread the things that deep
inside you wars
With peace and calmness, safety and still, you
might just discover
That within you lies a fear-stilling spirit, a
world-travel-lover.

Go search for mountain-top views and breezy
beach-bay days
Go find out where the middle of the middle-east
displays
Its golden temples, richest foods and people
silken robed

Where Asia keeps her rice stores, and fireworks
be strobed,
Where Africa holds the coolest air in the
shadows of a tree
Or the polar bears search for food in the ice-cold
baltic sea.

So take no notice of the things that people use to
scare you
You'll find the world is made up of many things
you never knew
And wouldn't have found out about
If you were to give in to all the doubt
Uncertainty is part of it, this life where we reside
But never let uncertainty be the reason you
never tried.

Covenant

Behind the faces, I've rarely seen
Within the places, I've seldom been
A simple truth, still somewhat hidden
Beyond a passion long forbidden

I see the sunrise on my dreams
And search in hope for what it means.
I ask the question often heard,
The one so many minds deterred.

The secret answer for which I long;
To understand where I belong.
Why does my mind so often stray?
Why can't these feelings keep away?

The answer comes through soft, but clear
When my heart whispers words that I fear:
It's in my blood, it's in my soul
This heritage I can't control.

My ancestors cry out to me
Myself to be, my heart set free.
A thousand miles from home I've traveled
My bloodline has so much unraveled.

Yet still at night, I smell the rain
And in my darkness feel the pain.
I must leave now, I must go back
And of my heritage keep track.

Years from now the world will know
The measures to which man will go
To prove his love, to keep his heart
And rue the times from home to part.

Then, softly, you will hear me say:
It's in my blood, I cannot stray.

Birthday Villanelle

Today would have been your birthday
There would have been chocolate cake
Old age should have come your way

There are so many things I still want to say;
A thousand memories I wanted to make
Today would have been your birthday.

Sometimes, it is hard to keep the tears at bay
So they fall, and I think that I can't help but
break
Because old age should have come your way.

It's hard for the ones who have to stay -
A struggle to smile sincerely, it seems so fake.
Today would have been your birthday.

I still light a candle for you and try to pray;
A ritual you taught me to take.
Old age should have come your way.

So we make tea and pretend we are okay
I'll keep going on for your sake
But today would have been your birthday.
Old age should have come your way.

The Watchman

The watchman, he watched intently from his
tower up on high
Above ramparts and turrets of Jericho on the
days before they came.
He kept his head over the crowd, he kept his
head, training his keen eye
His body ready for action, through the night he
remained the same.

The watchman, he watched intently from his
turret near the sky,
When he glimpsed a beauty, but knew not her
name.
With raven hair and angel lips, this creature
caught his eye.
And what could the watchman do then, for his
insides set aflame.

The watchman he watched, keeping vigil as she
continued on her way,
Drawing water as every other girl from the city's
deepest well.
He sought her out from the crowd as she
returned day after day.

So absorbed that he did not see the spies, he did
not ring the bell.

They came silently before him, this watchman
who looked away.
They rapped on a door in the wall,
And entered a house of shame.
The wanderers stayed safely and the woman
with feet of clay,
Fed them and hid them, then hung a cord from
the window frame.

Beyond the wood, an army was rising, ready to
make their way
Awaiting news from the house of a woman, set
in the city wall.
The army was waiting with patience, just
beyond the fray
The watchman did not see the thing that would
be his downfall.
The spies crept out at dawn, they tried to go
unseen.
They did not see the watchman, who waited out
of sight.
Without his beauty there, the watchman's eye
was keen
He raised the alarm in a flash, he rallied the
troops for a fight.

The watchman returned to his tower, ready at his
post.
The spies fortified their army, with the weapons
of their kind
When the time for battle drew near, they
remembered their host
The woman with the cord of scarlet whom they
left behind.

When the king demanded answers, the
watchman kept his tongue
In front of the royal advisors, he tied himself in
lies.
Yet the king had other watchmen, whose truth at
him was flung
The watchman was found guilty of not watching
for the spies.
He never saw his beauty, as his royal fate was
sealed
And he never heard the marching beyond the
city gate.
He did not see the axeman or the weapon he did
wield
As the noise rose up around him, the watchman
met his fall.

Autumn

At the bottom of my garden, where the gentle
breezes play
As the long and lazy branches of the wistful
willow sway
And the crisp autumn air's renewed chilling has
begun
When the sun cannot resist setting fire to the
horizon.

The air is filled with chattering and sparrows
taking flight
Practising for the big event of that long and
distant flight
No more summer air dwells among the bustling
bees
No more are children beckoning adventures in
the trees.
The woods are getting muddy, as the rains
increase their fall.

The trees around are bearing fewer leaves, as
they stand ever tall.

Flickering orange and red against the skies of
brightest blue,
And every one who notices adores the brilliant
hue
Against the blazing oranges of the oak and
maple's leaves.
So often we miss it, the subtle signs of life
As we focus so intently on our trouble and our
strife.
Too soon the birds will fly away, their formation
strong and great.
And we'll only really notice their presence when
it is too late.

Winter is before us, it is drawing ever near
But pay attention to this, for autumn now is here
Demanding in her temperament, howling in our
ears
Pouring down vast showers of icy, heavy tears.
Soon the branches will be empty of their friends
The birds, the leaves - in the end it all ends
Summer was a glory, but swiftly she has gone
Now, like those birds, we must focus ever on.

This Poem Does Not Rhyme

This poem does not rhyme
Often poems rhyme and I like it
I also like the rhythm of a nice
Iambic pentameter
Or a limerick
But there are many words that could
Rhyme with the last in the lines above
I think that you would be able to find
one for each and every last syllable if you tried

The rhythm - that's also not here
It would be fairly easy if I wanted to add it in

And just look at the disorder of each stanza,

They are not hard words to rhyme with
If you are giving it some thought
Except if I were to use words like...orange
And nothing properly rhymes with month.

This Place I know

Beyond the cobbled city lanes
A conversating voice aglow
Speaks of faces on the window panes.

Blazing lamps beside the street
cast eerie shadows high and low.
The light is caught upon her face

And though I think it quite discreet

The girl is of another place.

The men in pinstripe suits enquire,
"Has she then no home yet, sire?"

December's air is cold and clear
And yearns for brilliant adventure
That raises spirits and stirs up fear
Enveloping every folded heart
And brings promises it can't secure
Of snowflakes on the summer sun
The vow immediately falls apart
And hopes are once again undone.

The men in pinstripe suits enquire;
"Will this harm the future, sire?"

My faithful youth is terminated
As I look upon a bleak old man.
My pride is hereby confiscated
By my fingers on his beard that ran
Past my memory as I look behind.
I cast my mind back to his tragic goodbye
When he needed time, to search and find.

The men in pinstripe suits enquire,
"Did she not return here, sire?"

My prime has passed, and my children grown
Their little hands now holding mine
My memories with smiles they crown
And tears that somehow went astray
With a simple yet a witty line

That marks this moment forever blessed.
When I one day am gone away,
The glory of this place professed.

When men in pinstripe suits will comment
That life is none but fundament.

Haiku

Away goes summer
Flying on the icy breeze
Thank you for the sun.

Had We All The Time In The World

Had we all the time in the world, I would tell
you a thousand times
Of the times that I wanted to reach out and take
you by the hand
And run outside to stand in wait for the
churchbell when it chimes
Or run until we could run no more and find a
meadow to stand

With knee-high grasses and gasp at the poppies
all around
A million sleepy red flowers that grow so
wonderfully free
And laugh out loud as we fall out of breath to
the ground

Enjoying the sunny weather and happy with our
company

I would wake you up in the murmuring middle
of the stillest night
And say put on your warmest coat I've got
something to show you.
We'd sneak past creaky stairs lit by the dim
moonlight
And out to the darkness in the lawn and gaze up
at the view

The stars peeking out from the clouds that depart
The light as subtle pinpricks in the canvas of the
sky
And looking at you, I'd feel the beat of my heart
With you there, unaware, I'd let out a contented
sigh

Had we all the time in the world, I would have
had the chance
To be brave and tell you the things that I feel, of
why we should just choose to dance!

It's been a long time since you left our world,
the day you went away
Now I can only think of possibilities and how
they never may
Come to pass in a future together

How hard it is to think that I'll not see you. No,
not ever...

The Stubborn Mind

He wouldn't believe a letter
Of anything that was better
Than the thing that he said
Or the thoughts in his head
If she was right he'd still upset her

Gone

Everytime I see your face
And see you carry on
I recall my fears and once again,
Remember you are gone.

Gone forever from my grasp,
Gone into the future,
Leaving me behind.

My heart aches,
My breath struggles to come
As I remember you are gone.

Balance of Life

Everyone must play this game we call life
Easy are the pleasant times smooth and free
Harder the painful ones brimming with strife
How must we endure all the pain and the glee
Loving only makes it harder for sure
When there are so many more things to lose
Is it worth making it count to endure
Consequences hid behind what we choose
Then as one starts to give up hope in one's heart
Glitters a joy and delight never seen
Overshadowing the darkened part
The scarred remains of heartbreak had been.
Focusing on what matters after all
Remains the way to break this earthly fall.

Death, you've kept me company

Death, you've kept me company along the many years
Of blessed friends and family, sharing laughter, sharing tears.

You stayed by that summer's day that crept deep into the night
The heartbeat fell exhaustedly, giving up its fight.
The last breath that he took - as though only asleep.
We stayed nearby, as company his vigil wait to keep.

The next of those you took was harder than the first one
For though a father must be survived by his son
The rules do not apply the same for a brother
Death, you kept me company, watching our mother.
Her tears stayed away from people around
They stayed behind her mask: the grief too profound.

Not long did you dare to wait to see me once
more
Death you keep on taking more people than
before.
The elders and the wise ones, you took to your
side
You even took my cat, and watched on as I
cried.

Can you tell me death, which was the worst of
the lot?
I dare not even think the thought for if I do not
There may still be a chance to keep this one
nearby.
Thereby keep him closest still - it is clear why.

Goodbye then, death. For all that you have
taken.
In the years before I go with you, I hope you'll
be mistaken
If you think to take another one of those left
behind to me.
I release you then, dear friend. From my bond
you are set free.

The Tapestry of Life

Look how it knits together, this tapestry we call
life
With glorious joyful things and troubles that are
rife
Yet life is more than just this glimpse we see
before us now
So look at the many different times to work out
how
It all is woven in by the hand of a master
weaver.

He started weaving in the dark with breath
murmured to the night
Then out of the nothingness he spun a yarn of
purest light;

There in the moment between the two, the
weaver spun with grace
He spun fibre upon invisible fibre, knitting into
the night
The filaments and ligaments, the firmaments and
base.

He looked into the basest, barest bones of a
newly forming world,
Then sent them out into this place, he sent them
when they unfurled
The newly spun and woven strands of fish, of
bird and crawling beast
To creep and crawl and swim and fly from the
far west to the east.
A sudden din arose among them to this weaver
of them all.

Has Man ever stopped to listen, to the song that
they all sing
The song of stars and whales; the sound of a
hummingbird's wing?
Has Man ever stopped to see the way they
perfectly hold together
The neatly portioned packs of cells and the
proteins that they tether?
Then look how it all holds together! This
tapestry we call life.

For all this that exists before him, Man's focus is
not there
Too often he sees only the problems he must
bear
Humanity is swamped with its own ever human
grief
Too comfortable and too tempting to shed its
firm belief
Against a weaver that still is weaving an answer
to his call.

Procrastination

You've taken this down from a high-up shelf
And perhaps you are reading aloud to yourself
In a long silent room, with the household asleep
And the night-hours silently, onwardly creep

Flattering as it is to me, who wrote the words
you read
In a far distant place with a plan to fulfill an
amusing need
To bring something akin to a kinship on the
written page
A memory that spans across the years of many
an age

But you know as well as I do, that this was not
your task
And even if you do enjoy to read indulgingly,
still ask:
What was it that you meant to do, what are you
putting off?
Don't think that through the pages, I didn't hear
you scoff!

For even through the intervening years between
us two

You would do well to remember the things that
we both do
To read and write and write and read; these
things fascinate
So if you were to write your own, don't
procrastinate!

Close to Nature

Dear Daisy,

Today I saw a fox,
Running in the wild.
I saw a pheasant,
Flying in the sky.
I saw a little deer,
galloping away.
I saw a spiky hedgehog,
Trundling through the grass.

They were playing near a road;
They were frolicking in a field;
They were twirling in the twilit leaves
Of the autumn wind's first flurry.
And it brought happiness to me,
To see them being free.
Isn't it great that we can be so close to nature?

Dear Daisy,

Today I saw the fox again,
sleeping peacefully.
Not noticing one bit,
All the cars rushing by.

I saw the pheasant rising up,
Right before my eyes -
But I won't say what happened next,
It was a terrible surprise.

I saw the little deer again,
staring straight ahead.
It didn't even seem to see
The car coming with ghastly speed.
The hedgehog wasn't lucky again,
Trundling too, too near the edge when
I wish I could have stopped it all
The things that happened next.

Is it great that we can be so close to nature?

Soldiers On A Chessboard

The soldiers on the battlefield stood in forward
facing ranks
Their attention never waning from the threat that
lay ahead
With war laid out before them and rising on their
flanks,
The soldiers on the battlefield, so carefully did
tread.
A royal couple proudly stood, flanked on either
side,
By papal people, cavalry, the towers of defense.
And leading the way before them, every foot
soldier with pride
Strode in careful measure for the atmosphere
was tense.
Above them god-people of battle decided as they
went,
Ordering the army onwards, determined that
they win.
Even if it meant that to their death they may be
sent
And facing their opponents the bloodshed would
begin.

It started on the frontline with the footsoldiers
before,
On it went as battle raged throughout the
darkening hour
Advice from clergymen could not hold against
the corps
And defeat was almost certain, until there were
the towers;
Their straightened shots flew straight across
every rank and every file,
Making it impossible for the enemy to proceed.
Yet master of them all, driving fear through
every tile
Was the cold, composing power of the queen
who took the lead.

Terror spread as war raged on with fighting all
around
The lines were drawn, the boundaries formed in
black and white
The waging war raged unrelenting and both
sides lost their ground
As soldiers fell, cut down in the temper of the
fight
The lines were crossed. Ranks were lost.
So wars are waged and landscapes changed,
The best hope is an upward slope
That marks a change of heart and part

Renewed beginnings, black and white regardless
of the winnings,
Can live as one, and come undone
As soldiers on a chessboard.

The attempt counts

I did something hard and scary.

Today?

Well, I wanted to.

Today?

Well, I tried to.

Today?

Today.

Could you try again tomorrow?
The attempt counts.

The Willow and The Birch

The willow and the birch led very different lives
With different nature friends who played among
the chives
That grew in the earthy patch between their
sturdy trunks.
When eggs began to hatch within their
branching bunks,
The willow had hoards of insects that would
play
And the birch had only one solitary bird to stay
Wrapping on the trunk to hollow out his shelter
Ignoring the bees and wasps flying
helter-skelter.

Alone he pecked and chipped at his beloved
birch
Who did not mind at all and provided for him a
perch,
Where the woodpecker could watch his insect
neighbours
Both content with their little lot, and the end of
their labours.

Then as the weather turned, the rains began to
fall
The little bees and wasps did not like the wet at
all
They buzzed and busied on, to find somewhere
to be -
The only dry place around was in the
woodpecker's tree.
They entered through the gap; they settled on
every feather
The woodpecker could not breathe, with the
insects close together.
When the sun began to shine, the insects buzzed
with life
Out of the birch and back to their willow, the
smell of nectar rife
And though the willow swished her branches in
the lazy sun
The birch was left with a hole and its happiness
undone.

Final Salute

This is where we part,
the two of us who met
and dwelt within these pages.

I hope it gave you heart,
And if it did, may it yet
Be remembered through the stages

Of your life, the art
And the things that upset
And lead you through the ages.

9 789358 738421